Growing Up

Egg to Chicken

by Jodie Shepherd

EXPLORE
The LIFE
CYCLE!

Content Consultant

Lisa Monachelli, Education Director

Stamford Museum & Nature Center

SCHOLASTIC

Library of Congress Cataloging-in-Publication Data
Names: Kimmelman, Leslie, author.
Title: Egg to chicken / Leslie Kimmelman.
Description: New York: Children's Press, an imprint of Scholastic Inc.,
    2021. | Series: Growing up | Includes index. | Audience: Ages 6-7. |
    Audience: Grades K-1. | Summary: "Book introduces the reader to the life
    cycle of a chicken" — Provided by publisher.
Identifiers: LCCN 2020031788 | ISBN 9780531136959 (library binding) | ISBN 9780531137062 (paperback)
Subjects: LCSH: Chickens—Life cycles—Juvenile literature.
Classification: LCC SF487.5 .K56 2021 | DDC 636.5156—dc23
LC record available at https://lccn.loc.gov/2020031788

Printed in Heshan, China 62

SCHOLASTIC, CHILDREN'S PRESS, GROWING UP™, and associated logos are trademarks and/or registered trademarks of Scholastic Inc.

1 2 3 4 5 6 7 8 9 10 R 30 29 28 27 26 25 24 23 22 21

Scholastic Inc., 557 Broadway, New York, NY 10012.

Photos ©: 6: Auscape/Universal Images Group/Getty Images; 15 bottom: ands456/Getty Images; 16: Claus Lunau/Science Source; 18 left, center: Jean-Michel Labat/Biosphoto; 18 right: J.-M. Labat & F. Rouquette/Biosphoto; 19 left: Jean-Michel Labat/Biosphoto; 19 right: J.-M. Labat & F. Rouquette/Biosphoto; 21: Robert Pickett/Getty Images; 24 right: Cindy Sutton/Alamy Images; 26 center: Karl-Josef Hildenbrand/picture alliance/Getty Images; 27 top frizzle: FlamingPumpkin/Getty Images; 27 top silky: imageBROKER/Alamy Images; 27 center right: Régis Cavignaux/Biosphoto; 27 bottom: Bruno_il_segretario/Getty Images; 29 center right: Jean-Michel Labat/Biosphoto.

All other photos © Shutterstock.

Table of Contents

Wattle

Chickens don't sweat. Their blood cools down as it passes through the wattle.

Toes

Most chickens have four toes on each foot.

Claws

Chickens use their claws to scratch for food.

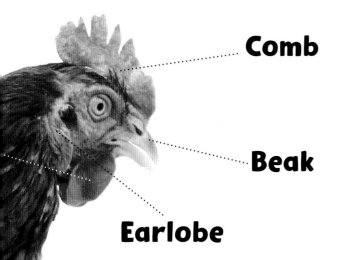

Comb

Beak

Earlobe

What Is a Chicken?

A chicken is a bird. All birds have feathers, two wings, and a beak. Like other birds, chickens like to eat insects, worms, and seeds. There are many different **breeds** of chickens. But they all begin their lives the same way: inside an egg!

Male chickens have larger combs than females do. ▶

Rooster

Hen

There are more chickens on Earth than humans!

Choosing a Partner

A female chicken is called a hen. A male chicken is a rooster. The hen is ready to have **chicks** when she is about 25 weeks old. She chooses a rooster for a **mate**. It will be the father of her chicks. She often chooses the rooster with the reddest, brightest comb and wattle.

Making a Nest

It is time for the hen to make a nest. She looks for a quiet, safe spot on the ground. The hen gathers twigs, feathers, and hay. She uses them to build the nest. Now she has a place where she can lay her eggs.

The hen spreads her weight evenly over the eggs so they don't break.

▼

Hens sometimes sing while they lay their eggs.

Laying the Eggs

The hen lays one egg a day for several days. She may lay seven or more eggs all together in a **clutch**. Then she sits on top of the eggs to keep them warm. That is when the chicks inside the eggs begin to grow. They will all be ready to hatch in 21 days.

Caring for the Eggs

The hen needs to make sure her eggs stay warm all over. She turns them over and over during the day. The hen rarely leaves the nest. If the eggs get too cold, the chicks growing inside may die. The mother hen also clucks to her eggs. She does this so the chicks will know her voice by the time they **hatch**.

A hen turns each of her eggs about 50 times per day.

Chicken Predators

The mother hen must also protect her eggs from **predators**. Many different animals will try to eat the eggs. Others may **prey** on the chicks after they hatch. Still other animals may try to catch and eat the full-grown hen, too.

Rats
eat the whole egg, including the shell.

Hawks
are strong
enough to carry
off an adult
chicken.

**Skunks
and foxes**
break the shell
open. They lick
out the insides.

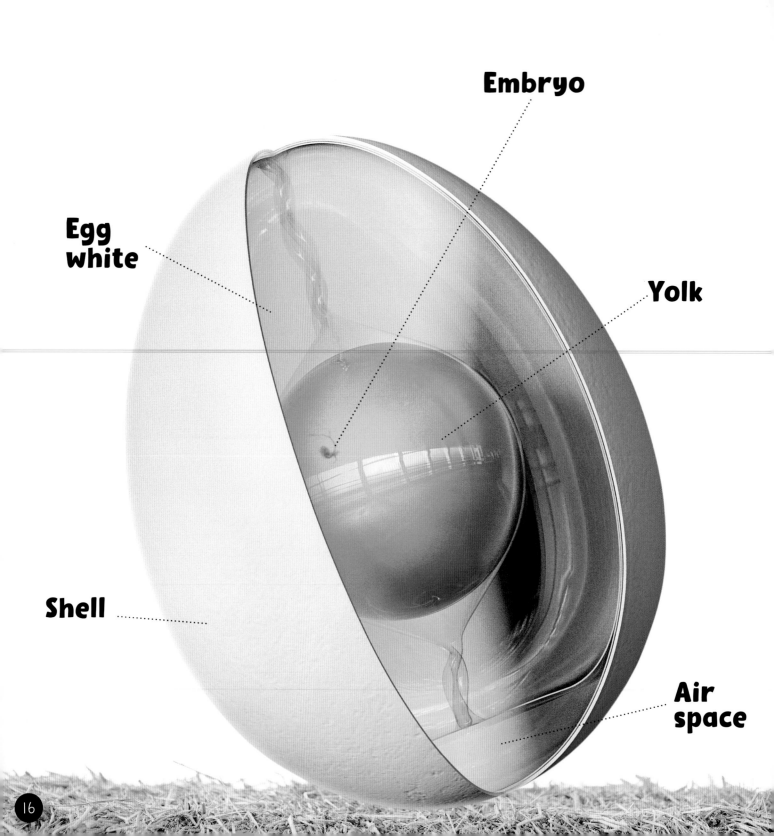

Embryo

Egg white

Yolk

Shell

Air space

Inside the Egg

A baby chick starts as an **embryo**. Everything the embryo needs to grow into a chick is inside the egg. The egg white is a cushion to protect the growing chick. The yolk is food for it to eat. There is an air space at the wide end of the egg. That will be the first air the chick breathes.

Hens with red earlobes lay brown eggs. Hens with white earlobes lay white eggs.

Beginning to Grow

At first the embryo is the size of a dot. It does not look like a chick at all. The embryo's body parts start to take shape within about 10 days. You can see its eyes and the beginnings

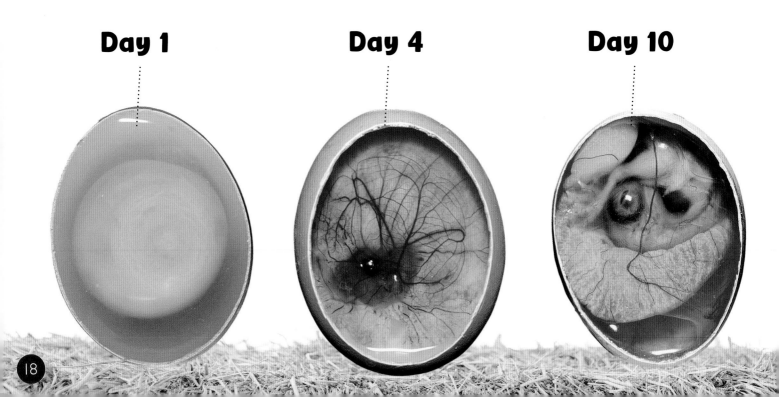

Day 1

Day 4

Day 10

of a beak. The chick's wings and legs are starting to form, too. By day 20, the chick will be taking up all the space in the egg. It can't grow any more!

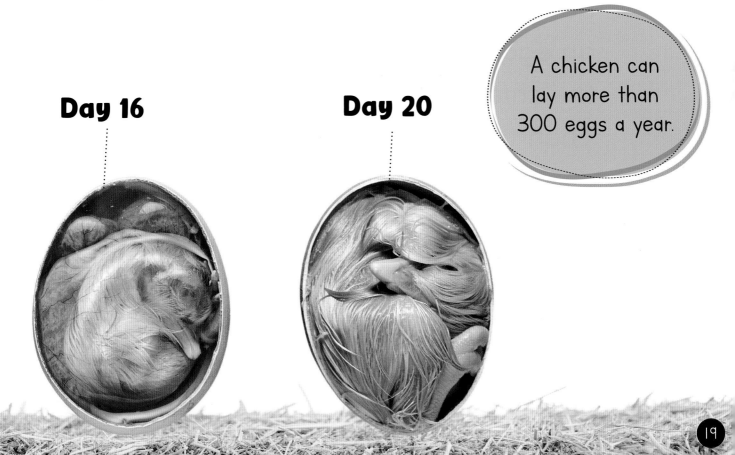

Day 16

Day 20

A chicken can lay more than 300 eggs a year.

No More Room

It's almost hatching time. The chick does not have a full comb or a wattle yet. But the rest of it is fully formed. Soft feathers called **down** cover its body. It has a bump on its beak called an egg tooth. The egg tooth will help the chick **peck** its way out of the shell. Then the egg tooth will fall off.

By the time the chick is ready to hatch, the yolk is almost all gone.

Egg tooth

It can take up
to 24 hours for a
chick to break out
of its shell.

▼

Hatching Time!

A cheeping noise is coming from inside the egg. The chick is ready to hatch! Next the chick begins to peck and peck. It is hard work. It may take thousands of pecks to crack the shell open. Finally, the chick hatches. It is wet, weak, and wobbly.

All the chicks in a clutch hatch within 24 hours.

Growing Up

Just one day after hatching, the chicks are already active. They can walk, run, and scratch for food. At six or seven days old, they begin to grow real feathers. They will still have some

Two days

Six days

down until all their feathers come in. By eight weeks, the birds look like adult chickens. Some may grow up to be roosters. Others may be hens. One day they will lay eggs of their own!

Five weeks

A very young hen is called a pullet. A young rooster is called a cockerel.

Chicken and Egg Facts

Because their eyes are on the sides of their heads, chickens can see almost all the way around. They can also see in more colors than humans.

Chickens can fly, but they don't fly far. Their wings are too small to carry their bodies for long.

All birds grow from an egg. Chicken eggs are larger than songbird eggs. But they are much smaller than ostrich eggs. One ostrich egg (left) is equal to about 24 chicken eggs (right).

There are many breeds of chickens. Most look similar, but Silkies (right) have fluffy, silky feathers. Frizzles (left) have curly feathers.

Different chicken breeds may lay white, brown, blue, red, or even speckled eggs. They are all the same on the inside.

Roosters have a toe-like growth on each leg called a spur. The spur has a sharp claw on the end and is used for self-defense.

Red jungle fowl are the chicken's wild **relative**. The birds are **native** to the jungles of India but have spread all over the world.

Growing Up from Egg to Chicken

A chicken starts its life as a tiny embryo inside an egg. It goes through many changes as it grows into an adult.

Adult
By eight weeks, the chicken has a full set of feathers, a comb, and a wattle. By about six months, a hen can begin laying eggs, and the cycle starts all over again!

Egg
Like all birds, chicken embryos develop inside an egg.

Embryo
It grows inside its egg for about 21 days.

Chick
At about six or seven days old, the chick will begin to grow its first feathers.

Hatchling
The newborn chick is called a hatchling at first.

Glossary

breeds (BREEDZ) particular types of plants or animals

chicks (CHIX) very young birds

clutch (KLUHCH) a nest of eggs

down (DOUN) the soft feathers of a bird

embryo (EM-bree-oh) a baby human, an animal, or a plant in the very early stages of development before birth

hatch (HACH) when an egg breaks open and a bird, reptile, amphibian, insect, or fish comes out of it

mate (MATE) the male or female partner of a pair of animals

native (NAY-tiv) living or growing naturally in a certain place

peck (PEK) to strike or pick up something with the beak

predators (PRED-uh-turz) animals that live by hunting other animals for food

prey (PRAY) to hunt and eat another animal

relative (REL-uh-tiv) a family member

Index

About the Author

Jodie Shepherd, who also writes under her real name, Leslie Kimmelman, is an award-winning author of dozens of fiction and nonfiction titles for children and was a longtime editor at Sesame Workshop. She loves both chickens and eggs and has spent a long time pondering which came first.